PUFFIN BOOKS
AMMA, TAKE ME TO THE TAJ MAHAL

Bhakti Mathur took to writing in 2010 when she created the popular *Amma, Tell Me* series of children's picture books about Indian festivals and mythology. After a long stint as a banker, she now juggles her time between her writing, her passion for yoga and spending time with her family. She lives in Hong Kong with her husband, their two children and two dogs. She holds a master of fine arts in creative writing from the University of Hong Kong, is a freelance journalist and contributes regularly to the South China Morning Post. She is also a life and career coach. When not writing or running after her young boys, Bhakti is happiest curled up with a book in one hand and a hot cup of chai in the other. To learn more about her, visit her at www.bhaktimathur.com and www.reflectwithbhakti.com.

Priyankar Gupta is an animation film designer and visual storyteller. He is associated with various publishing houses as an illustrator for children's books and also works as a pre-visualizer for TV commercials and feature films. He is a visiting faculty member and mentor in various design institutes across the country.

Also in Puffin by Bhakti Mathur

Amma, Take Me to the Golden Temple

Amma, Take Me to Tirupati

Amma, Take Me to the Dargah of Salim Chisti

Amma, Take Me to Shirdi

Amma, Take Me to the
Taj Mahal

BHAKTI MATHUR
Illustrations by Priyankar Gupta

PUFFIN BOOKS
An imprint of Penguin Random House

For Anurag, Shiv and Veer

PUFFIN BOOKS

USA | Canada | UK | Ireland | Australia
New Zealand | India | South Africa | China

Puffin Books is part of the Penguin Random House group of companies
whose addresses can be found at global.penguinrandomhouse.com

Published by Penguin Random House India Pvt. Ltd
4th Floor, Capital Tower 1, MG Road,
Gurugram 122 002, Haryana, India

First published in Puffin Books by Penguin Random House India 2022

Text copyright © Bhakti Mathur 2022
Series copyright © Penguin Random House India 2022
Illustrations copyright © Priyankar Gupta 2022

ISBN 9780143451648

Typeset in Agmena Pro
Printed at Aarvee Promotions, India

www.penguin.co.in

CONTENTS

1. Tomb 2. Mosque 3. Guest house 4. Yamuna river 5. Ornamental pools

6. Main gate 7. Forecourt 8. Servants' quarters 9. Royal tombs

AUTHOR'S NOTE

The *Amma, Take Me* series is an attempt to introduce children to the places of historical interest and different faiths in India. Styled as the travelogues of a mother and her two young children, these books link history, archeology, tradition and mythology to bring alive the major monuments of India in an engaging and informative way.

The stories emphasise universal values and the message of love and tolerance central to all faiths. They seek to make children aware about India's unique cultural heritage. I hope that this journey of Amma and her children will inspire you to embark on your own travels with your children, and I hope that you will enjoy reading these books as much as I enjoyed writing them.

Lastly, these works are a reflection of my personal interpretation of the faith and traditions that these timeless monuments represent. I am far from being an authority on religion or history, and while I have made every effort to ensure factual and historical accuracy, I do not assume and hereby disclaim any liability to any party for any loss, damage or disruption caused by errors or omissions in these books.

Bhakti Mathur

Amma, Shiv and Veer stood at the Great Gate, the *darwaza-i-rausa*, the main entrance of the complex. A monumental rectangular structure with a facade of red sandstone and white marble, it rose imposingly above them, 30 metres high and 40 metres wide. A tall central doorway in the shape of an arch was flanked by two smaller stacked arches on both sides, and two beautifully ornamented gates. Octagonal towers topped with white marbled domes stood at the four corners of the edifice and on the top of the frame of the central doorway, sat a row of eleven small white marbled cupolas.

The three walked through the passageway, and as they emerged, they stopped in their tracks, stunned by the sight that lay ahead of them. They had seen it many times before, in photographs and from a distance as they had driven into the city, but still, were unprepared for the breathtaking beauty of the vision that greeted them.

A platform of red sandstone floated above the riverbank, on which rested a spacious terrace of white marble. From the terrace rose a shimmering white marbled structure of flawless symmetry, crowned with a rounded dome and framed by four tapering minarets. The platform lifted the structure in a way that it was silhouetted dramatically against the turquoise blue sky, beyond. Majestic in its beauty, the monument seemed suspended between heaven and earth. It seemed to float, almost weightless above its surrounding courtyards, mirror like water courses and emerald gardens.

Amma, Shiv and Veer stood in silence for a few moments, soaking in the sight of the most beautiful mausoleum in the world, the Taj Mahal.

Finally, Amma broke the reverie.

'Every time I see the Taj Mahal, it looks more beautiful than before,' said Amma.

'How many times have you been here, Amma?' asked Veer.

'This is my fifth visit,' replied Amma.

'Fifth!' exclaimed Shiv.

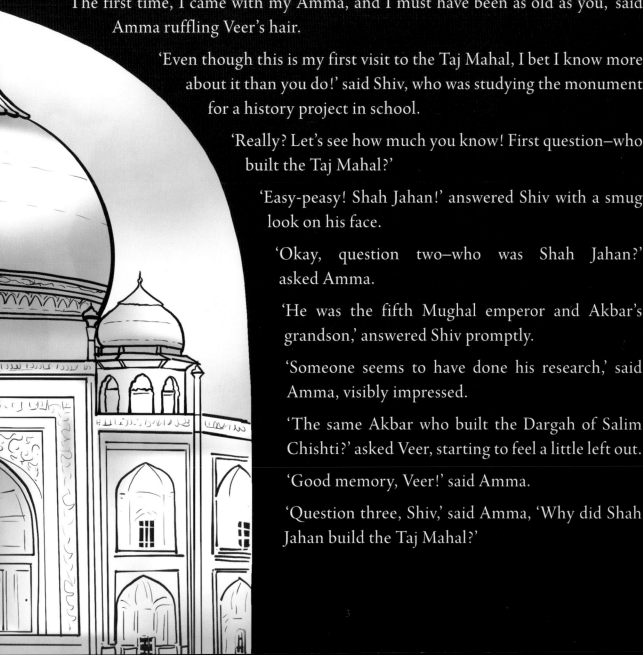

The first time, I came with my Amma, and I must have been as old as you,' said Amma ruffling Veer's hair.

'Even though this is my first visit to the Taj Mahal, I bet I know more about it than you do!' said Shiv, who was studying the monument for a history project in school.

'Really? Let's see how much you know! First question—who built the Taj Mahal?'

'Easy-peasy! Shah Jahan!' answered Shiv with a smug look on his face.

'Okay, question two—who was Shah Jahan?' asked Amma.

'He was the fifth Mughal emperor and Akbar's grandson,' answered Shiv promptly.

'Someone seems to have done his research,' said Amma, visibly impressed.

'The same Akbar who built the Dargah of Salim Chishti?' asked Veer, starting to feel a little left out.

'Good memory, Veer!' said Amma.

'Question three, Shiv,' said Amma, 'Why did Shah Jahan build the Taj Mahal?'

3

'He built it as a tomb for his wife Mumtaz Mahal, after her death. He loved her very much and wanted to build it to keep her memory alive for ever. She is buried here, and so was he after his death. It took 22 years to build and was completed in 1653. Almost 8 million tourists come to see the Taj Mahal every year, and it is one of the seven wonders of the world,' Shiv rattled on, eager to show off his knowledge.

'You are right, Shiv,' said Amma. 'Let's see if you can name the other wonders of the world.'

'Hey, how is that a question about the Taj Mahal?' asked Shiv. 'But let's see, the other wonders are the Great Wall of China, the Colosseum in Rome, Machu Picchu in Peru.' He paused and scratched his head for a few seconds and gave up. 'I don't know what the rest are.'

'They are the Khaznah in Petra, Jordan, the statue of Christ the Redeemer in Rio de Janeiro and a pyramid called El Castillo in Mexico,' said Amma.

'I want to visit them all!' said Veer.

'I am one up on you. I've been to the Great Wall of China and you haven't!' Shiv teased Veer.

'Stop teasing your brother, Shiv,' said Amma. 'Shall we go closer now or sit on this bench to soak in this view of the Taj Mahal for some more time, while I tell you a story from its past?' asked Amma.

'Very clever, Amma. You know we never say no to a story,' said Veer, grabbing her hand, and pulling her towards the white marble bench next to them.

The two boys sat with Amma between them, and they looked up as the morning rays of the sun fell on the mausoleum, bathing it with a soft red glow. A few people stood near them gazing at the monument in awe, while a tour guide explained the history of the tomb to another group. A young couple who looked newly married, posed for selfies with the Taj Mahal as their backdrop.

'The story of the Taj Mahal does not start with Shah Jahan,' said Amma, 'It begins 170 years before the mausoleum was built.'

'What do you mean?' asked Shiv.

'This story begins in the year 1483, in a tiny kingdom called Ferghana, nestled in the mountains of Central Asia. This was in the country of Uzbekistan. Celebrated for its orchards and its gardens, Ferghana was a beautiful valley, flanked by hills, and where two rivers merged into the Syr Darya river. It was ruled by a king called, Umar Shaikh Mirza. Umar Shaikh was brave, good-natured and fun to be with. He had a son whom he named, Zahiruddin, which means "Defender of the Faith".

The young Zahiruddin liked to crawl and pretend to be a tiger, and so his father started calling him "Babur", or "tiger" in Persian. So he came to be called Zahiruddin Muhammad Babur.

Umar Shaikh loved pigeons and had a dovecote built, high on the walls of his fortress, which was situated on the edge of a ravine.'

'What is a dovecote, Amma?' asked Veer.

'A dovecote is a small enclosure for doves and other birds to live in,' explained Amma.

'One day, Umar Shaikh was up in his pigeon house feeding the birds, when the ancient walls of his castle crumbled causing Umar Shaikh to fall to his death.'

Shiv and Veer gasped.

'And so Babur, who was only twelve years old at the time, became the ruler of Ferghana.'

'He was as old as me!' said Veer. 'I can be a king too!' he exclaimed raising his hands in the air.

Amma and Shiv started laughing.

'Wait a second. Is he the same Babur who won the war at Sikri? You told us his story when we went to the Dargah of Salim Chishti,' Veer's eyes sparkled.

'Yes, indeed he is the same Babur,' said Amma. 'But his most famous battle is the one that he fought a few years earlier—the Battle of Panipat.'

'Tell us more!' chimed Shiv and Veer together.

Amma continued with the story. 'Young Babur was surrounded by many powerful enemies who wanted to claim his father's throne. So his hold over Ferghana was under constant threat.

Yet, young Babur was ambitious and dreamt of becoming a famous conqueror. He was after all, a descendant of the legendary Genghis Khan, a great soldier and general, who founded one of the largest empires in the world—the Mughal Empire.

In fact, the word Mughal comes from 'Mongol'. Genghis Khan was born in Mongolia in 1162 and founded an empire that stretched from China across Central Asia to Europe.

Babur was the great-great-grandson of Timur, another legendary conqueror. Born in Uzbekistan in 1336, Timur was part Mongol and part Turk. His empire stretched from the borders of China to Turkey, with the thriving city of Samarkand as its capital. After conquering Central Asia, Timur went on to invade northern India. A proud descendant of Timur, Babur dreamt of following in his footsteps.'

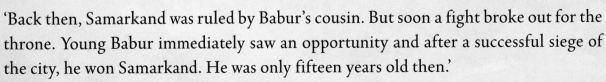

Shiv and Veer listened wide-eyed.

'Back then, Samarkand was ruled by Babur's cousin. But soon a fight broke out for the throne. Young Babur immediately saw an opportunity and after a successful siege of the city, he won Samarkand. He was only fifteen years old then.'

'That must have been such a proud moment for Babur!' said Veer.

'It was,' affirmed Amma 'but he didn't get enough time to savour his success. A few nobles back home in Ferghana rebelled against him, and placed his younger brother on the throne there. When Babur marched to reclaim Ferghana, he lost Samarkand as well and was left with nothing.'

'Oh no! What did he do, Amma?' asked Shiv.

'For the next six years, Babur constantly fought to win back Ferghana and Samarkand, but failed. He was forced to look elsewhere. He saw an opportunity when his uncle, the ruler of Kabul, died. With the help of a band of loyal followers he was able to capture the city. Babur was 21 years old when he became a king again.'

'I know Kabul,' said Veer excitedly. 'It's the capital of Afghanistan. That's where Rashid Khan is from.'

'That's right, Veer! The famous leg spinner,' said Amma.

'Go on, Amma. What happened next?' asked Shiv.

'Inspired by the conquests of his ancestors, Babur turned his gaze towards Hindustan. From 1519 to 1525, he led five expeditions into India and finally succeeded in his last attempt. In October 1525, he marched with 12,000 soldiers across the Khyber Pass onto the same wide plains in northern Hindustan that Timur had conquered over a century ago.

By February 1526, Babur had advanced far into Punjab. His army had grown to 25,000 soldiers, as he gathered allies and reinforcements, along the way. However, the numbers under his command were still small in comparison to the army of Ibrahim Lodhi, the Sultan of Delhi, who had 100,000 soldiers waiting to vanquish the invader.'

'You mean for every soldier that Babur had, Ibrahim Lodhi had four!' exclaimed Shiv, doing a quick calculation.

'That's right. Not only that, Lodhi's army also included a battalion of 1,000 armoured elephants!' said Amma.

'What happened next?' asked Veer eagerly.

'Till then, Babur had fought most of his battles in hilly regions, in constrained battlefields, where large forces could not be deployed. It was not the size of the army but the strategic use of land that was crucial in winning those combats. However, Babur was now in the plains, in open country, a battlefield he was not accustomed to. Babur thought hard, "What do I need to do to win this war?"'

'So, tell us, how did he win?' asked Veer, impatiently.

'Babur summoned a meeting of his generals and a plan was made to negate the advantage of Lodhi's larger army. Once Babur reached the outskirts of Panipat, he deployed his army between the town to the right and the Yamuna river to the left. The houses and buildings of the town, protected his right flank. To protect his left flank, he asked the soldiers to dig deep trenches and make a barricade of felled trees between their position and the river. This narrowed the width of the field and ensured that the battle was fought along a narrow front. Lodhi's larger force would have no chance to sweep around and outflank Babur's smaller army.'

'Babur planned such a clever strategy!' exclaimed Shiv.

'To protect his frontline, Babur ordered his men to gather as many carts as they could find. His soldiers set up a barrier of 700 wagons, placed four meters apart, joined together with ropes of rawhide, so that it became a long chain. In between the carts, Babur placed his gunmen and his cannons in such a way that they could not be seen by the enemy.

You see, Babur had laid a trap, a long corridor with houses on one side and ditches on the other with gunmen hidden in the middle. It took Babur several days to provoke Ibrahim Lodhi into attacking his prepared position, but finally Lodhi's army attacked, galloping fast, to overrun the Mughals.

Squeezed between the walls of Panipat on their left and Babur's ditches on the right, the Lodhi army found itself in a bottleneck as it closed in on the Mughals. The Mughals fired their canons, frightening the soldiers and the elephants. Soon Lodhi's forward divisions faltered and tried to rein in, but the ranks behind were unable to break their momentum, and slammed into them, throwing the entire army into disarray. Lodhi's formations were taken by surprise, unable to fight or retreat, exactly as Babur had planned.

The battle was won by Babur and his army, within five hours. By noon, 20,000 soldiers of Lodhi's army were killed and Ibrahim Lodhi himself was slain.'

Shiv and Veer shuddered.

'But Babur was a man of principles. "Honour to your bravery!" he exclaimed and called for a brocade cloth to shroud Ibrahim Lodhi's body. He ordered two of his top commanders to bury the Sultan with full honour at the spot where he had fallen.'

'That was kind of him!' said Veer.

'Indeed, it was,' said Amma. 'With this great victory Babur ended the reign of the Delhi Sultanate that had ruled over a large part of Hindustan for more than 300 years. He became the most powerful ruler of Hindustan and made Agra his capital. This was the start of the Mughal empire in India. So, you see, without Babur, there would have been no Taj Mahal.'

The three of them were silent for a while as they stared at the beautiful symmetry of the water channels and the gardens that stretched in front of them. A long canal, flanked by alleys paved with red sandstone, ran from the Great Gate to the base of the mausoleum. It intersected in the middle of the garden at a right angle with another canal, dividing the grounds in four congruent squares.

At the intersection of the canals, stood a wide ornamental pool of white marble. The waterways and the pool were studded with fountains. Decorated with lotus patterns, the canals and the pool reflected the Taj Mahal and the tall, elegant trees. It was difficult to say which looked more beautiful—the tomb or its reflection. One could spend the entire day watching the colours change in the reflecting waters as the sun rose and set.

'Look there's a pool in the middle! Let's see who reaches it first!' said Veer, dashing off towards it.

'Wait!' said Amma, but the two had raced ahead.

'This is no place to run,' Amma chided them, as she caught up with them a minute later, a bit out of breath.

Standing in front of the marble pool, the three now had a better perspective of the structure of the gardens around them.

'Do you notice something special about the gardens?' asked Amma.

Shiv and Veer looked intently.

'I'll give you a hint, it's got to do with a shape,' said Amma.

'I got it!' said Veer.

'Squares! There are four squares!' said Shiv just as Veer was going to answer.

Veer rolled his eyes at Shiv.

'Wrong!' said Veer. 'There are sixteen squares.'

'Veer is right!' said Amma.

Now it was Shiv who glared back at Veer.

'Okay, okay, both of you are right,' said Amma. 'There are four squares, each divided into four smaller squares making a total of sixteen squares. We are standing in the middle of what is called a *chahar* or *char bagh*, meaning, a fourfold enclosed garden. *Chahar* means four and char baghs were brought to India by Babur.

Within each of the sixteen quarters of the *char bagh*, colourful flowerbeds were planted. The flowerbeds were divided by raised stone pathways. Trees lined the pathways providing shade from the sun.

These trees that you see,' said Amma pointing ahead are cypress trees which were brought by the Mughals to India. They originally came from Persia, or modern-day Iran, and were considered a symbol of eternity. The history of these gardens dates back 2,500 years,' said Amma enjoying the serenity of the gardens.

'I thought the Taj Mahal was built 450 years ago?' asked Veer.

'It was, but this particular design of gardens is from an earlier time,' said Amma 'One of Babur's first acts as an emperor was to create a beautiful garden on the opposite bank of the Yamuna, where the Taj Mahal stands now.'

'Really! Is it still there?' asked Shiv.

'Can we go see it?' said Veer.

'Only traces of the garden remain now,' said Amma.

'Building a garden may seem an unusual activity for a warrior, but for Babur it was a natural thing to do. Designing gardens was his passion and he was a genius at it. It was a talent he inherited from Timur who created *char baghs* so beautiful that they were called "paradise gardens". Do you know where the word "paradise" comes from?' asked Amma.

The boys shrugged.

'From an old Farsi word, *pairidaeza*, which means a "walled garden". In both Christianity and Islam, gardens are linked to the image of heaven or paradise. Persians were the greatest gardeners of the ancient world. Their walled gardens provided privacy and peace from the dust and discord outside. Water features intersected in the centre of the garden and were used for irrigating sections of the garden which were full of flowering trees,' explained Amma.

'Just like the gardens here,' observed Shiv.

'Correct!' said Amma.

'When Timur invaded Persia, he borrowed the idea of paradise gardens and incorporated it into the gardens with which he surrounded his capital city of Samarkand. Within the garden walls, he created a luxurious encampment of extravagantly decorated pavilions that befitted his status as a conqueror. While Timur moved his nomadic encampment from garden to garden, he had his throne fixed on a platform above the spot where the watercourses representing the four rivers of life crossed, a symbol of his dominion over the four quarters of the world.'

With that fascinating history on paradise gardens, Amma allowed the boys to soak in the magnificent view.

'The Quran implies that paradise is a series of terraces, holding splendid gardens. The gardens here are symbolic of the paradise that Shah Jahan wanted to create for his beloved Mumtaz.'

Shiv and Veer listened with rapt attention.

'Water was essential to irrigate the gardens, fill its fountains, channels and pools. Do you know how these gardens were irrigated?' asked Amma.

Shiv and Veer shook their heads.

'To ensure a dependable water supply, the builders captured and stored water from the Yamuna in three large reservoirs that were built on a high support outside the garden wall. From there it was released into channels that were buried beneath the garden. These channels delivered water effortlessly across the *char bagh*.

Storing and releasing water was the easy part. The tough part was to get the water from the Yamuna up to these storage tanks. It had to be raised to a height of 50 feet and transported 900 feet.'

'How did they do that?' asked Veer.

'With the help of buffaloes', answered Amma with a smile.

Shiv and Veer looked puzzled.

'An aqueduct was built to feed the water of the Yamuna to the reservoir tanks. Water buffaloes did the hard work of raising the river water to the top of the aqueduct, from where the water flowed to the tanks,' explained Amma.

'What is an aqueduct, Amma?' asked Veer 'and how did the buffaloes raise the water?'

'An aqueduct is a channel built to move water,' said Amma. 'Workers standing below the aqueduct scooped water from a tank connected to the river into leather buckets. Each bucket was harnessed by a long rope to a water buffalo. When a bucket was full, a worker at the top of the aqueduct sent the water buffalo down a ramp on the far side. As the water buffalo walked down, the bucket was pulled up to be emptied into the aqueduct. When the enormous animal trudged back up the ramp, the empty bucket dropped down into the tank and the process began again.'

'How clever!' said Shiv.

'Yes, indeed! The Taj Mahal is an immense engineering achievement wherever you look,' said Amma.

'Coming back to the gardens that Babur built,' said Amma. 'Cool and breezy, the *char bagh* gave Babur relief from the unrelenting heat and dust of his new home. It became the centre of his life. In the middle of the garden, he built a pavilion where he relaxed and wrote his diary. He planned military campaigns, held public audiences, composed music and poetry and entertained his friends, all in his gardens. Babur's diary became his extraordinary autobiography, the *Baburnama*, a warm and candid memoir, from which we get to know much about Babur and his life.'

'How cool, Babur wrote a diary!' said Shiv.

'Yes, we have it at home. You can read it once we get back,' said Amma and carried on.

'Unfortunately, Babur got very little time to enjoy his new kingdom and his gardens. He died just four years after his victory at Panipat in 1530. After Babur's death, his son Humayun succeeded him but, he too, like his father, lost control of his empire. After battling for 15 years he regained the Mughal throne in 1555, but just after seven months, Humayun fell off the steps of his library and died. His 13-year-old son and heir, Akbar, was crowned emperor.'

'I know Akbar! His name means "The Great," said Veer. 'He sought the blessings of Salim Chishti and had the Dargah built in his honour!'

'Yes! The same Akbar!' said Amma and went on. 'It was Akbar who stabilized the still shaky Mughal empire and ruled for 49 long and prosperous years. When he died in 1605, he left a vast and powerful empire to his son Jahangir who in turn ruled for 22 years.

The sixteenth and seventeenth centuries are one of the most fascinating periods in Indian history, when the country was ruled by the extraordinary Mughal emperors. The period from 1526 to 1657 includes the reigns of the first five: Babur, Humayun, Akbar, Jahangir and Shah Jahan. In sometimes bloody, but uninterrupted succession, the Mughal dynasty produced five generations of outstanding rulers with many diverse talents: they were men of action, refined diplomats, excellent judges of character and lovers of art and music.'

'The Mughal emperors were so talented!' said Veer.

'Yes, they were and historians regard them as India's most flamboyant rulers ever. They built beautiful and lasting monuments. Their passion and appreciation for art, literature and music led to a cultural enrichment. Their tolerance for all religions and faiths and their sophisticated system of administration brought stability to a greater part of India.

At their zenith, the Mughal emperors ruled over 150 million people, a quarter of the world's population at the time. Their empire included most of what is India, Pakistan, Bangladesh and part of Afghanistan today. Their capital was Agra.

What the Mughals achieved was quite remarkable as they were foreigners in the land they had conquered. They were also Muslims, while most of their subjects were Hindus. However, the Mughals did not let this difference come in the way of building an empire. While they had the threat of a powerful army at their disposal, they also understood the importance of diplomacy. They appointed Hindus to important government positions and even adopted Hindu traditions and celebrated Hindu festivals. They forged important alliances with the Hindu princely states by marrying Hindu princesses, and elevating Hindu noblemen, artists and workers to important positions in their court.'

'One of Akbar's wives was Hindu,' said Shiv.

'That's right Shiv, not one but many,' said Amma.

'By the time Shah Jahan ascended the throne in 1628, Agra was one of the greatest cities in the world, with an estimated population of 7,50,000 people. Everything precious or rare in the world could be found in its bazaars. It was a haven for scholars, artists, artisans and craftsmen from all over the country. The Mughal empire was one of the wealthiest empires in the world and historians say that Shah Jahan was the richest man in the world!'

'Like Jeff Bezos and Elon Musk!' said Veer.

BABUR   HUMAYUN   AKBAR

JAHANGIR   SHAH JAHAN

'You could say that,' laughed Amma.

'Shah Jahan was Emperor Jahangir's third son. He was born on 5 January, 1592, in Lahore, in present-day Pakistan. His mother, Jagat Gosain, also known as Jodh Bai, was a Rajput princess from Marwar. There was much happiness and celebration at his birth. You know, what is interesting is that although Shah Jahan was brought up as a Muslim, he had Hindu lineage,' said Amma.

'How is that?' asked Shiv.

'Because his mother and his father's mother were both Hindu,' replied Amma.

'On the sixth day of his birth, the little prince was given the name "Khurram" meaning "joyous" in Farsi by his grandfather Akbar. Just before his birth, a fortune teller told Ruqaiya Sultan Begum, Akbar's first wife, that the child would have a great future and be more resplendent than the sun. Ruqaiya Begum did not have any children, so, when Khurram was just six days old, Akbar ordered that the little prince be given to Ruqaiya, so that she could bring him up.'

'Khurram's Amma must have been so sad,' said Veer, sporting a long face.

'Yes, she must have been,' said Amma. 'But Ruqaiya loved Khurram with all her heart, and raised him like her own son. When Akbar died in 1605, the young prince was re-united with his mother. Khurram, like all children in the Mughal empire, grew up in the palace harem.'

'What is a harem?' asked Veer.

'The word 'harem' comes from the Arabic word 'harim', which means a sacred or forbidden place. It is a domestic space, reserved for only the women and children of the family. It was home to the women of the royal family—mothers, aunts, sisters and cousins. The only man allowed to enter the harem was the emperor himself. It was also where the royal children were brought up.'

'Why is that Amma?' asked Veer.

'It was a custom for a woman to cover her face with a veil when she appeared in public, but inside the harem, the women were free to take off their veils. The royal harems offered all kinds of comfort and luxuries. It had schools, markets and playgrounds.

In the palace harem, "Baba Khurram", as he was affectionately called, was pampered and spoilt, but outside it he received a great education. Famous scholars, poets and Sufi mystics taught him religion, literature, history and music. He was well versed in the history and tradition of his famous ancestors and trained to become a warrior. Khurram loved sports and became an excellent sportsman, passionate hunter and an excellent shot.'

'What sports did they play back then?' Shiv asked eagerly.

'Well, Khurram's sports were a bit different from yours. He loved horse riding, shooting and hunting and taming wild elephants!' said Amma. 'But I am sure he would have been a good cricketer, too, had the game existed then. He was very athletic.'

'Maybe, but he wouldn't have been able to bowl as fast as me!' said Veer.

Amma and Shiv looked at each other and started laughing.

'Khurram was very close to his grandfather, Akbar, who showered him with affection. Akbar even took the boy with him to the battleground to teach him military strategy. At the age of nine, Khurram joined his grandfather's war council,' said Amma.

'That's two years younger than me!' quipped Veer. 'I can go to battle too.'

Amma rolled her eyes and continued.

'After Akbar's death, Khurram's father Salim was proclaimed emperor and took the title "Jahangir" meaning "King of the World". Meanwhile, Khurram continued with his education. But when he was 15 years old, his life changed.'

'Why, what happened?' the boys asked in unison.

'He met a girl and fell in love,' said Amma.

'Who was she?' asked Veer

'Where did he meet her?' asked Shiv.

'Hold on you two, one by one!' said Amma and continued.

'Her name was Arjumand Banu and she was fourteen years old at the time. Shah Jahan saw her at a royal bazaar during the celebrations for the Parsi new year called *Navroze*. The bazaar, known as the Meena Bazaar, was set up in the fragrant gardens of the Agra Fort, where the emperor resided. The gardens were lit with candles, and coloured lanterns swayed from the branches of the trees. The wives and daughters of the nobles set up stalls selling silk and velvet garments, brocades, jewellery and exotic cosmetics. They bantered and bargained with their purchasers, the emperor and his family and friends. This festive occasion was one of the few times that the women were allowed to drop their silken veils and reveal their faces in public.'

'Like in the harem,' said Veer.

'I am glad you have been paying attention,' said Amma. 'Arjumand Banu was selling glass beads at a stall, when Khurram saw her and the young prince could not keep his eyes off her. He stopped at her kiosk and bought a large piece of glass, shaped like a diamond. He is said to have paid ten thousand rupees for this–an incredibly high price. Arjumand was equally entranced by the young prince.'

'Was she a princess?' asked Veer.

'She was the granddaughter of Mirza Ghiyas Beg, a Persian nobleman who joined the Mughal court when Akbar was emperor and had risen to become Jahangir's finance minister. Her father Abdul Hasan Asaf Khan was the grand vizier to Jahangir and her mother was a Persian noblewoman. Interestingly, her aunt, Nur Jahan, married Jahangir and exercised a powerful influence on the emperor. Arjumand grew up in the palace harem.

Arjumand and Khurram fell in love and the prince asked his father for permission to marry her. His father agreed on one condition, Khurram had to wait five years and during that time he could not meet Arjumand Banu.'

'Why is that?'asked Shiv.

'Maybe because the prince was too young. He was just one year older than you, Shiv,' said Amma. 'Perhaps, Jahangir wanted to see if Khurram was serious about her or if it was just a teenage crush. Maybe he had other reasons—who knows! Anyway, a lot happened during those five years. One such event was Khurram's marriage to a Persian princess upon his father's insistence.'

'Why did he marry someone else?' asked Veer.

'He didn't have a choice. He had to listen to his father, the emperor. Sometimes emperors arranged marriages for political reasons to strengthen their ties and form alliances with other kingdoms,' explained Amma.

'However, even while they were apart, the love between Khurram and Arjumand Banu only grew stronger and deeper. So, when the five years were up, Khurram reminded his father of his promise. Jahangir remained true to his word and in May 1612, the young couple were wed in a grand ceremony.

In true Mughal style, the wedding was celebrated with great pomp and show. Before the ceremony, the womenfolk of the family painted Khurram's hands with henna and turmeric for good luck. Jahangir tied a marriage tiara of glittering pearls upon his son's forehead. Next, the young bride gave her formal consent to be wed and gifts were exchanged between the two families. Fireworks illuminated the sky, and the feasts and celebrations lasted for a month.

The prince was 20 years old at the time and his new wife was 19. Khurram gave her the name "Mumtaz Mahal" meaning "Jewel of the Palace". The wedding was the beginning of their wonderful life together. From that day on, Mumtaz Mahal was Khurram's constant companion, his trusted advisor and the love of his life.

Khurram could not have been happier. He had married the woman of his dreams and was his father's favourite son and heir apparent,' said Amma.

'Just like me! I am Dad's favourite, too,' said Veer.

'In your dreams,' retorted Shiv.

'Even though Khurram had two older brothers, Jahangir awarded him the territory of Hissar Feroza in Punjab and the right to pitch a crimson tent, an honour that was traditionally conferred on the emperor's chosen heir. Jahangir became more and more dependent on Khurram and entrusted him with all his major military campaigns. Though Jahangir was an excellent administrator, he had little interest in waging wars and conquering new lands. He drank excessively and was addicted to a drug, opium.'

Shiv and Veer gasped.

'Why did he do that?' asked Shiv.

'It's hard to say why. Whatever the cause, addiction is never good and it certainly led to Jahangir making some very poor decisions, which led to his eventual downfall,' said Amma and continued.

'Khurram was a great soldier and a commander who was loved and respected by his men. He led his troops to put down rebellions against the Mughal empire, especially in the Deccan region of India. Going on long campaigns with the army was hardly customary for a princess, but Mumtaz insisted upon traveling with her husband, wherever his duties took him. Despite the danger to her, she remained by his side at all times and twelve of their fourteen children were born during such expeditions.'

'What! They had fourteen children!' squeaked Shiv. 'That's more than a cricket team.'

'With a few extras,' added Veer.

'Oh, it's always cricket with you two,' said Amma.

'In those days, people had many children, especially kings and noblemen to ensure that they had successors to their titles and their lineage. Also, back then, the death rate among infants and children was very high so not many lived to become adults. Only seven of Mumtaz and Shah Jahan's children survived,' explained Amma.

'That's sad,' said Shiv. The three were silent for a few minutes, taking in their surroundings once again.

It was past noon by now. The afternoon sun's rays shone on the mausoleum, making it glisten and dazzle, looking like a jewel against the opaque blue of the skyline. The mausoleum appeared to have changed colour from morning to afternoon, the sun's rays reflecting off the marble, which was faintly streaked in pale shades of grey, tan and white, giving the marble a unique quality.

Amma was engrossed, admiring the beauty of the mausoleum when Shiv's voice broke her reverie.

'I want to go inside the mausoleum!' said Shiv.

'Me too!' said Veer, tugging at Amma's saree.

'Wait,' said Amma, 'There's one more story I want to tell you both, and then I promise we will go inside.'

The three sat down on the lawn. The perfectly proportioned dome of the white mausoleum rose majestically in front of them.

'I want to tell you about the Mughal expeditions. Mughal emperors spent a large part of their reign on the move, on battles and campaigns, conquering new lands,' said Amma. 'A Mughal army on the move was a majestic sight. First to appear were the cavalry columns. Next in line were the marching infantry in their green silk uniforms, followed by elephants, bedecked in golden cloth, clanging with gold and silver plates and bells. The artillery arrived next, with great bronze cannons pulled on wooden gun carriages by teams of bullocks.'

'Wow!' said Veer in awe.

'Some of the canons had barrels as long as seventeen feet and one of these barrels was Shah Jahan's favourite which he named "conqueror of the world". Next came thousands of camels, mules and ox-drawn carts. Finally came the emperor, the royal princes and their bodyguards, along with the musicians playing long-stemmed pipes, trumpets and kettledrums. Tens and thousands of attendants and camp followers straggled behind.'

'I want to go on an expedition like this!' said Veer.

'You can't travel back in time, can you?' joked Shiv.

Amma carried on with the story.

'Mumtaz and Shah Jahan occupied a large, fort-like enclosure in the centre of the camp, well protected by artillery and fences. The outer walls of their pavilion consisted of panels of wood draped with scarlet cloth. Within the enclosure were some of the facilities of the royal court, like tented halls shimmering with gold and silver fabrics where Shah Jahan, seated under a velvet canopy, would meet his officers and his scouts.'

'This sounds like a moving palace!' said Shiv.

'Indeed, it was,' said Amma. 'These camps were born out of meticulous planning and hard work. The *Akbarnama*, which is the official chronicle of the rein of Akbar written by his court historian Abu'l Fazl, says that it took 100 elephants, 500 camels and 400 carts to transport the tents and camp equipment of a Mughal imperial campaign.'

Shiv and Veer were enthralled.

'Shah Jahan led countless expeditions. In 1617, on one such campaign, the prince quelled a threatening uprising against the Mughals in the Deccan. Jahangir was proud of his son. On his return, the emperor showered him with precious jewels and gold coins and proclaimed that henceforth the prince be known as "Shah Jahan", meaning, "Lord of the World". Shah Jahan had proven himself to be a capable general and a diplomat and was the chosen successor to the Mughal throne in all but name.'

'But, just as things could not have been better for Shah Jahan, his fortunes took a sinister turn. Remember, I mentioned that Jahangir had married Nur Jahan— Mumtaz Mahal's aunt.'

Shiv and Veer nodded.

'Nur Jahan had become extremely influential in Jahangir's court as the emperor became more addicted to wine and opium and spent less and less time in matters of the court and the administration of his empire. Nur Jahan saw the emperor's reliance on Shah Jahan as a threat to her growing power. She was sure that his succession to the Mughal throne would cause an end to her growing influence. Nur Jahan was too ambitious to resign herself to the quiet life of a widowed empress after Jahangir's death. Historians believe that she plotted to get her daughter—Ladli—from a previous marriage, to be engaged to Shahryar, Shah Jahan's younger brother. She wished to support Shahryar's claim to the Mughal throne, in a bid to sideline Shah Jahan.

This angered Shah Jahan, who had been declared as the next in line to be emperor. Fearing that the clever Nur Jahan was about to convince Jahangir to name Shahryar as his heir, a furious Shah Jahan revolted against his father. The troops of both father and son clashed, with over 50,000 soldiers in battle. Shah Jahan's army was overpowered. He was defeated and had no choice but to implore his father for forgiveness.

Jahangir agreed to forgive him on two conditions: Shah Jahan and Mumtaz were sent away to live in exile and they had to leave two of their sons, ten-year-old Dara Shikoh and seven-year-old Aurangzeb with Jahangir as hostages.'

Shiv and Veer looked visibly shaken.

'Amidst all this, Mumtaz, remained steadfastly by Shah Jahan's side, sharing the hardship of exile, just as she had shared the glory when Shah Jahan was still the favoured son.

In 1627, Jahangir died after a long illness. Shah Jahan was still in exile and there were many rivals for the throne. But, even before his father died, the prince had begun clearing the path to the crown. Three of his brothers, two nephews and two cousins died, including his younger brother Shaharyar and his half-brother Khusrau. Historians say that most were murdered on Shah Jahan's orders.'

'Is this true Amma?' asked Shiv, shocked.

'Apparently, it is. There is a famous Mughal proverb, *takht ya takhta*, which literally means "throne or coffin". It suggests that either you claim the throne or you risk losing your life. By ordering his brother Khusrau's murder, Shah Jahan had committed an act that would haunt his reign and establish a violent precedent among his children. Violence was common in those days. It was how battles were won, lands were conquered and empires were established. Still, Shah Jahan's actions were brutal by any standards. As fate would have it, Khusrau's murder would come back to haunt Shah Jahan.'

'What do you mean, Amma?' asked Veer.

'We will come to that later,' said Amma and smiled. 'Shah Jahan was crowned emperor on 14 February, 1628, seventy-two years after his grandfather Akbar's succession to the throne, and 145 years after his great-great grandfather Babur's birth. He was the happiest, he had been in his life. He had the riches of the world at his feet and his beloved Mumtaz by his side. He was 36, at the prime of his life, with no threats to the throne.

Shah Jahan was an excellent administrator. He was able and conscientious in his duties, and he retained a tight control on every aspect of his huge empire. He had an insatiable passion for architecture, and was one of the most prolific builders of the Mughal empire. He was a self-taught, yet gifted architect. His buildings were unmatched in beauty, balance and design, and his works represent the height of Mughal architecture. Among the great monuments that he built are the Jama Masjid in Delhi, one of finest mosques in India, the beautiful Moti Masjid or Pearl Mosque inside the Agra Fort, the Red Fort in Delhi and the Shalimar Gardens in Lahore.

One of his first acts as emperor was to commission the Takht-e-Taauus, the famous 'Peacock Throne', to display the most splendid gems in the imperial collection. Shah Jahan's knowledge of gems and jewels was extensive and his collection was probably the most magnificent in the world at the time. He selected the precious stones himself from the seven treasure houses spread across his empire. The treasury at Agra alone held 750 pounds of pearls, 275 pounds of emeralds and corals and countless other semi-precious stones.'

Shiv and Veer listened wide eyed.

'In fact, the biggest and the most famous diamond in the world "The Kohinoor" belonged to Shah Jahan and was embedded in the Peacock Throne.'

'The same Kohinoor that we saw in London?' asked Shiv.

'Good memory, Shiv. Yes, we saw it in the Tower of London,' said Amma.

'How did it get to London?' asked Veer.

'Smart question, Veer,' said Amma. 'The history of the Kohinoor is captivating. Let me tell you about it. After Babur defeated Ibrahim Lodhi, he seized the treasury at Agra, which had the great Kohinoor Diamond. It is said to have weighed 240 carats and was as a big as an egg.'

Shiv and Veer's jaws dropped.

'Babur wrote in the *Baburnama* that the Kohinoor was so valuable that it could feed the entire world for two and a half days.'

'Wow, how many people would that be?' asked Shiv.

'The world had 500 million people in the 16th century,' replied Amma. 'Compared to almost 8 billion, today.'

'Wow, that's an increase of more than 15 times over 500 years!' exclaimed Shiv.

'Stop showing off your math skills, Shiv,' said Veer, annoyed.

'The Kohinoor passed on to the successive Mughal emperors. In the early 18th century, Nadir Shah of Persia invaded Delhi and looted its treasures, including the Peacock Throne. However, he was unable to find the enormous diamond and was informed that Muhammad Shah, the Mughal emperor, had carried it away, hidden in his turban. The clever Nadir Shah invited the Mughal to a feast during which he proposed an exchange of turbans as a gesture of friendship. The emperor was forced to comply.'

Shiv and Veer were riveted.

'What happened next?' asked Veer.

'Nadir Shah looked for the gem in the folds of the turban and there it was. The huge oval stone blazed with such brightness that he is said to have exclaimed "It is a Kohinoor, a mountain of light!"'

The boys were silent as Amma continued with the story.

'It was believed that the Kohinoor would bring the owner either the power to rule the world or great misery. For Nadir Shah, the diamond certainly brought bad luck. He and his sons were assassinated, and Nadir Shah's grandson Shah Rukh was forced to give up the famous heirloom to Ahmad Shah, the ruler of Afghanistan. After Ahmad Shah's death, two of his surviving sons fled to Punjab with the diamond.'

'So, it came back to India?' said Veer.

'Yes, for a short period of time. Maharaja Ranjit Singh, the ruler of Punjab obtained the stone from the Afghans. After Ranjit Singh's death, his empire disintegrated. The British forces defeated the Sikhs in 1849 and the diamond became a property of the British empire. The Kohinoor was presented to Queen Victoria as a historic symbol of her sovereignty over India. Queen Victoria wore it in a tiara and a brooch and later it was set in a crown for Queen Mary. So that is how the most famous diamond in the world ended up in London,' said Amma.

Shiv and Veer were silent for a while.

'What happened to the Peacock Throne, Amma?' asked Shiv.

'Shah Jahan worked closely with his jewellers to design the throne which was eight-feet long, six-feet wide, twelve-feet high and surmounted by a jewelled canopy. It took seven years to build and cost Shah Jahan almost twice as much as the Taj Mahal would.'

Shiv and Veer gasped.

'How much did it cost?' asked Veer.

'We'll come to that soon,' said Amma.

'It is said that diamonds, pearls, rubies and emeralds weighing 230 kilograms and 1150 kilograms of gold were used to make the throne. It had steps leading up to it, giving the impression that the ruler floated above the ground, closer to heaven. When

Shah Jahan, sat on the throne, he could only be seen by a small number of courtiers, aristocrats and visiting dignitaries.'

'Why was it called the peacock throne?' asked Veer.

'On top of each pillar there were two peacocks set with gems, and between each of the two peacocks was a tree set with rubies, diamonds, emeralds and pearls. According to Islamic belief, the peacock was once the guardian to paradise. The ruler's court was said to represent paradise on earth and inscribed at the back of the throne were the words, "If there is a paradise on earth, it is here, it is here."

Everything about Shah Jahan from his demeanour to his attire and jewels, was carefully designed to project grandeur and magnificence. Shah Jahan wore lavishly embroidered, full-skirted coats of silk and brocade and tunics of fine muslin or satin. Though he was not very tall, Shah Jahan was powerfully built, broad-shouldered and barrel chested—a wheat complexioned, handsome man with a sharp, chiselled nose, a tight mouth, large heavy-lidded eyes, arched eyebrows and a broad sweep of forehead.

Shah Jahan's daily routine was interesting. His day began two hours before dawn, when he awoke in his residence at the Agra Fort overlooking the Yamuna river. He washed and prayed for the first of five times. As the sun rose, he appeared to his people on the *jharokha-i-darshan*, which means the "balcony of viewing", jutting out over the sandy banks of the Yamuna below. The emperor's daily appearance, known as "darshan" allowed the public to freely voice their needs and desires.

While the masses assembled beyond the fort walls and gazed up at their emperor, he amused himself by watching furious elephants parading on the riverbank below, or the antics of jugglers and acrobats.'

'How do you know that?' asked Shiv. 'Did he write a diary like Babur?'

'Shah Jahan did not write a diary. However, he selected writers to chronicle the accounts of his reign. All that we know about him, come from these reports.

Next, Shah Jahan proceeded to the hall of public audience, where his officials awaited him. Mumtaz watched and listened through stone grilles built into the wall as her husband dealt with petitions, reviewed reports and received gifts. After about two hours, the emperor retired to the hall of private audience with his senior advisers to discuss important matters of state and receive foreign ambassadors and to dispense justice to the oppressed.

Common people came to tell him their grievances, and ask him for help. On his birthday, he had himself weighed four times. The first time, the scales

were balanced against silver coins, the second time against gold, the third time against cloth woven with gold, silver and silk. All of these were then distributed among the people.'

'Amma, just like we saw in Tirupati!' said Shiv.

'Yes! Remember the little girl being weighed on the gigantic scale with her sitting on one side, and sacks of rice on the other measure?' said Amma.

Shah Jahan sought Mumtaz's advice on key matters. Mumtaz had no political ambitions but was politically astute and was known to influence Shah Jahan, particularly in issues that women were facing. She had a soft, discreet approach and relied on her Persian friend and attendant, Satti al-Nisa Khanan, to bring to her attention cases of underprivileged girls and women in need. She placed these cases before the emperor, who ordered grants to be given to them. Shah Jahan granted her the official seal, the *Muhr Uzah*, which conferred on her the right to review official documents in their final draft form, a rare privilege for a woman. Mumtaz was influential but did not control Shah Jahan. She was, in every sense, his equal.

At night, the emperor returned to the harem for the evening meal. The nights would be filled with music and stirring melodies and sometimes, Shah Jahan would play chess with Mumtaz. The chess pieces were made of ivory, sandalwood, silver or gold.

'Wow!' said Shiv.

'I like Shah Jahan! He played chess like me,' said Veer. 'You think I could have beaten him?'

'I'm not sure about that,' said Amma, patting his back.

'Shah Jahan's peaceful reign did not last very long. In 1631, three years after his coronation as emperor, there was yet another uprising in the Deccan. Khan Jahan Lodi, the governor of the Deccan for the Mughals, had revolted. Shah Jahan embarked on yet another military campaign to quell the rebellion, travelling to the city of Burhanpur, in Madhya Pradesh, which served as the Mughals' command centre for their battles in Southern India. Burhanpur lay on the Tapti River, 450 miles southwest of Agra.

As always, Mumtaz travelled with her husband, even though she was pregnant with their fourteenth child. Shah Jahan and Mumtaz knew Burhanpur well, they had spent a large part of their married life here, and three of their children were born in the city.

The imperial retinue reached the city and settled down in their fortress, known as Shahi Qila, located on the banks of the river Tapti. While Shah Jahan consulted his commanders and considered his war strategy, Mumtaz rested in the royal apartments. Shah Jahan had created a haven for Mumtaz in the fortress. Red lilies and sweet scented champa flowers bloomed in the courtyards and fountains sprayed cool water. He had a hammam built, so that Mumtaz could enjoy luxurious baths.'

'What is a hammam, Amma?' asked Shiv.

'Hammam means a bathhouse. Shah Jahan had a royal bath constructed for his queen to relax in. It had a rectangular hall made of marble with domed roofs, with a large octagonal bathing pool in the middle, in which Mumtaz would enjoy a bath in water, scented with rose petals and saffron. The ceiling was decorated with beautiful paintings. The frescos though flaked and fading now, reveal an exquisite palette and one of these images depicting a domed structure with minarets is said to have been the architectural inspiration for the Taj Mahal.'

'Is that true Amma?'

'It's hard to say, but the image does seem to resemble the Taj Mahal,' said Amma.

Most of the fortress is in ruins but the hammam remains,' said Amma.

'Can we go see it?' asked Veer.

'We'll have to travel to Burhanpur for that,' said Amma 'and there's so much to see here!'

'Yeah, Veer,' said Shiv rebuking his younger brother. 'What happened next, Amma?'

'In the intense heat of summer, Mumtaz went into labour and after an agonizing thirty-hour long labour, she gave birth to a daughter named Gauhar Ara. The long labour made Mumtaz Mahal very weak as she had lost a lot of blood. She was convinced that she did not have long to live and she sent Jahanara, her eldest daughter, to hurry and fetch Shah Jahan to her side.

A weeping Mumtaz said, "I am dying, I know it. I must have these final precious moments with you. You must not spend your life in regret. Take care of our children, love them like I did." Saying this, the queen died in his arms. She was only 38 years old.

Shiv and Veer were silent.

'Historians recount another story about Mumtaz's dying words to Shah Jahan. They say that as Shah Jahan cradled his dying wife in his arms, she said, "I have one more thing to ask of you. In my dream, I've seen a white marble palace, luminous as a great pearl, in the midst of a lush garden. Build me such a resting place, where you and our children can come to visit me"' Amma said.

'Shah Jahan promised to create a paradise for Mumtaz, tears streaming down his face. Mumtaz Mahal looked lovingly at Shah Jahan for one last time and left the world.'

'So which story is true?' asked Veer.

'There's no way of knowing that' said Amma. 'And it does not matter. What is true is that Mumtaz Mahal was the love of Shah Jahan's life, and the Taj Mahal stands witness to their love.'

'Mumtaz's death broke Shah Jahan and he was never the same again. The emperor went into mourning and donned white clothes instead of his brilliant robes and jewels.

He would continue to wear these for the next two years, and thereafter on every Wednesday, the day of Mumtaz's death. He did not appear on his balcony, nor in the halls of private and public audience for a full week. When he reappeared in public, he looked old and haggard, even though he was just 39 years old. His hair and beard which hardly had any grey hair earlier, turned white within a few days.'

Shiv and Veer looked sad.

'His vision became so bad from constant weeping that he needed spectacles. He postponed the wedding of his sons Dara Shikoh and Shah Shuja, which he had planned along with Mumtaz. Eventually he allowed his eldest daughter, Jahanara, to spend time with him and she was a great solace to her father, sharing his grief.

Shah Jahan never intended Burhanpur to be Mumtaz's permanent grave. He had already started planning a fitting monument for his Queen. Perhaps this idea is what kept him going during the months after her death. In December 1631, a melancholy procession set out from Burhanpur to bring the dead empress home to Agra. It was led by Shah Shuja, her fifteen-year-old son who rode ahead of a formation of horsemen and elephants, with his mother's body in a golden casket atop an elephant. People lined the streets across villages and towns to view the procession as it journeyed the 900 kilometres to Agra. Holy men recited verses from the Quran and royal attendants distributed gold coins to the poor along the way.'

Shiv and Veer were listening quietly.

'The procession reached Agra in January 1632 and Mumtaz's body was buried at a location near the Yamuna. Shah Jahan named the tomb *Rauza-i-munavvara*, meaning "the illuminated tomb", which people simply called "rauza".

The bank of the Yamuna was perfect as the empress's permanent resting place. It was peaceful and away from the bustling centre of Agra with easy access to water needed to irrigate the gardens that would surround it. In fact, the banks of Yamuna outside Agra were lined with elegant, luxurious mansions of noblemen, with their flower filled, tree-shaded gardens. More than forty *char baghs* had been built along the Yamuna since Babur's time. But, of course, the Taj Mahal had to dwarf them all.

Shah Jahan chose a place along the Yamuna with a dramatic bend in the course of the river, which made it the perfect setting for the planned mausoleum. But he encountered a slight problem.'

'What problem did he face, Amma?' asked Veer.

'A residence belonging to Raja Jai Singh, the ruler of Amber, present-day Jaipur, stood at the site. Raja Jai Singh had inherited the land from his grandfather Raja Man Singh, a friend of Akbar's and one of the first Rajput allies of the Mughal court. Jai Singh was ready to gift the property to Shah Jahan, but the emperor did not want to take a favour for the land on which the empress' resting place was to be built. So, he gave Raja Jai Singh four other mansions in Agra in exchange for the land,' said Amma.

'The idea for Mumtaz Mahal's tomb may have begun as an expression of love and grief, but in true Mughal fashion, the plans for the project became larger and grander. Shah Jahan's passion for architecture and his perception of monuments as a symbol of power motivated the designs for the Taj Mahal as much as the emperor's love for Mumtaz.'

'Do you know how the Taj Mahal gets its name?' asked Amma.

Shiv and Veer shrugged.

'Some say it's an abbreviation of Mumtaz Mahal's name. However, since "Taj" means crown, it could also have been named to mean the Crown of all Palaces,' said Amma.

'The construction of the Taj Mahal began in 1632 and a ceremony to mark Mumtaz's first death anniversary was held at the construction site on 22 June, 1632. This was the *Urs* ceremony.'

'Like the *Urs* celebration of Sheikh Salim Chishti that you told us about?' asked Veer.

'That's right!' said Amma, looking pleased. '*Urs* literally means marriage in Arabic but also refers to death anniversaries since death is considered to be the union of the soul with God.'

'Mumtaz's first *Urs* was a sombre yet lavish affair. Tents were raised in the gardens and hundreds of people attended the event. Shah Jahan, who was still in mourning, appeared in white robes. Mumtaz's remains were moved to her final resting place in the Taj Mahal, a year later in 1633, and from then then on, every year on her death anniversary, an *Urs* ceremony was held for her. A lot of the information about the construction of the Taj Mahal comes from the written accounts of these anniversary celebrations.'

'The construction of the Taj Mahal took 22 years. So which year was the construction completed by, Veer? 'asked Amma.

'Amma, please stop with the irritating math questions. I am not in grade two anymore,' said Veer, annoyed.

'Okay, you math genius,' Amma smiled and continued. 'The mausoleum itself was almost finished by 1648, work on the gardens and the ancillary buildings lasted for a few more years and the grand project was finally completed in 1654.'

Amma, Shiv and Veer got up from their perch in the garden by the central pool and started to walk towards the mausoleum in front of them. The magnificent marble tomb with its pear-shaped dome seemed to grow larger and towered above them as they approached nearer.

A mosque built of warm red sandstone stood to the west of the mausoleum.

'The mosque was built as a place of worship for visitors to the tomb,' explained Amma.

'Look, there's one just like it over there,' said Veer, pointing to the opposite side of the mausoleum.

'That's not a mosque. It served as a guesthouse for visitors and the designers added it to give symmetry to the complex,' explained Amma.

Four identical minarets, some 30 meters high, stood at the four corners of the raised platform framing the main mausoleum between them. They were all topped by dome shaped canopied pavilions.

'Minarets are slender towers, typically part of a mosque, with a pavilion from which a muezzin calls Muslims to prayer,' explained Amma. 'Though the minarets seem upright, if you look carefully, you will notice that they are leaning away from the mausoleum. This was done so that they would fall in the opposite direction of the mausoleum and not damage it, in the event of an earthquake,' said Amma.

'There is another reason that the minarets were made to lean outwards. It has to do with an optical illusion,' said Amma.

'What does that mean?' asked Veer.

'Optical illusions are images that our eyes perceive differently than what they really are. This was first discovered by the ancient Greeks when they built their many pillared temples like the Parthenon. They found that perfectly straight columns seemed slightly concave to the human eye. To rectify this, they made columns that were slightly convex.'

'One of the special things about the Taj Mahal is that it is an amalgamation of ideas from many different styles of architecture. The setting at the end of a *char bagh* has

Persian and Timurid roots. The high arched doorways and the pear-shaped domes that you see here are common to monuments in Central Asia. However, the domed kiosks and the canopied pavilions, called *chattris,* as well as the intricate stone carvings are inspired by Hindu architecture of the time. In some ways the Taj Mahal reflects the assimilation of Shah Jahan's Persian and Hindustani heritage and the result is this perfect harmony of bulbous domes, vaulted gateways, massive halls, minarets and elaborate ornamentation.

One of the greatest achievements of the architects was to produce an elegant double-dome design for the mausoleum,' said Amma. 'What you see from here is the main outer dome, but there is a separate inner dome as well, which we will see from inside the mausoleum. The inner dome rises 80 feet high. What is cool is that the inner dome is perfectly proportioned to the main inner chamber while the outer dome is in perfect proportion to the exterior of the complex.'

'Can you guess how much the dome weighs?' asked Amma, looking upwards.

The boys shrugged, looking clueless.

'12,000 tons!' said Amma. 'That's the weight of 2,000 elephants put together!'

'Woah!' said Veer.

'The dome is almost 60 metres above the ground. Given how much it weighs and how high it is from the floor, imagine how difficult it would have been to construct it. It is an engineering marvel,' said Amma.

Shiv and Veer looked in wonder.

'This grand domed structure had been used only once, in a burial site, in India and that was in the tomb of Humayun, the emperor's great grandfather.'

'Where is Humayun's tomb?' asked Shiv.

'In Delhi,' said Amma.

'What does that look like?' asked Veer.

'It is beautiful as well and is believed to be an inspiration for the Taj Mahal as there are many design similarities between the two mausoleums,' said Amma and continued.

'Over the years as the Mughal empire grew larger and wealthier, the emperors became more extravagant as each tried to outdo their previous generation in both the lavishness of their lifestyles as well as the monuments they left behind.

When Babur died in 1530, he was laid to rest at a garden he had designed at Agra, called Char Bhurji, meaning "four minarets", on the opposite bank of the Yamuna from where the Taj Mahal would rise a century later. A few years later, around 1543, following Babur's wish, his remains were sent to Kabul to be buried in his favourite garden that overlooked a stream and a vast meadow. It stands to this day as a simple grave open to the sky and overlooking the small kingdom that Babur regarded as his home.'

'Where is Akbar buried, Amma?' asked Shiv.

'In contrast, Akbar is buried in a grand tomb, built on 119 acres of land, not very far from here in a place called Sikandra,' said Amma.

Coming back to the Taj Mahal, one of the outstanding features of the mausoleum that makes it stand out from the other Mughal buildings is the symmetry of its design.

'What do you mean, Amma?' asked Shiv.

'For once, if you imagine a vertical straight line through the middle of the arched doorway facing us, the left and the right of the mausoleum are mirror images of each other,' said Amma.

Shiv and Veer looked up at the mausoleum in front of them and then slowly turned left and right. They then turned around to see the gardens and the canal leading back to the Grand Gate from which they had entered the complex, judging the symmetry of the structure for themselves.

'Wow, you are right, Amma', said Shiv with amazement. 'It is perfectly symmetrical.'

'Well, there's more,' smiled Amma. 'If you measure the height of the mausoleum and compare it to the length and its width, you will realise that it is designed as a perfect cube. Another example of the symmetry is in the dimensions of the central domed building and the four minarets in relation to each other. Look carefully and you will notice that the first storey gallery of the minarets is aligned with the first floor of the mausoleum, their third-storey gallery is level with the top of the drum on which the central dome sits. The cupola of the minarets is aligned with the maximum bulge of the dome,' said Amma.

Shiv and Veer looked carefully, their eyes moving from the dome to the minarets and back.

'These architects were clever, and they had a thorough knowledge of mathematics and geometry,' explained Amma.

'Can you guess how many workers it took to build the Taj Mahal?' asked Amma.

'I know, 22,000!' replied Shiv.

'Very good! You seem to know your facts!' said Amma. 'It took 22,000 labourers, 1000 elephants and huge teams of buffaloes and donkeys.

Shah Jahan summoned workers from all over the empire. The best builders and craftsmen of the empire were recruited. Bricklayers, gardeners, stonemasons and carpenters flocked in, by the thousands. Shah Jahan built a city to the south of the construction site, in order to house all the workers. He fittingly named it Mumtazabad.

First the site was cleared and hillocks in the surrounding areas were levelled. The workers, who had only hand tools to work with, carried excavated materials in baskets on their heads.'

'This must have been hard work, especially in the harsh summers,' said Shiv.

'Yes, it was. Mughal mausoleums were traditionally built at the exact centre of a *char bagh*, but as you can see that is not the case with the Taj Mahal. The tomb here is at the edge of the garden, overlooking the Yamuna. It was an unusual decision by Shah Jahan and a risky one,' said Amma.

'Why was it risky?' asked Veer.

'Because there was a chance the Yamuna could flood in the monsoons as it often did,' replied Amma. 'Perched at the edge of the river, the Taj Mahal would be in danger of being washed away by the flood waters.'

'Did the Taj Mahal ever get flooded?' asked Veer.

'Never in its history, thanks to the clever builders,' said Amma.

'Oh wow! What did they do?' asked Veer.

'Let's walk up the platform and I will explain,' said Amma.

The three reached the base of the massive platform. It was decorated with delicate carvings. The top of the plinth was accentuated by a carving of a row of leaves hanging from stems. The stems were intertwined and above them hung, acanthus buds.

Amma and the boys walked up the steps that led them to the top of the gigantic platform which was about 300 metres long and 120 metres wide.

For a while, none of them spoke.

'Amma, tell us what the builders did to prevent the Taj Mahal from getting flooded,' asked Shiv.

'By making this platform on which we are standing,' replied Amma.

'What do you mean?' asked Veer.

'This platform elevates the Taj Mahal high above the river,' said Amma. 'Right now we are standing on what used to be the riverbank. A big challenge that the builders faced was to lay a foundation that would hold a platform. Imagine building such a huge one on the sands of the riverbed! But the builders came up with an idea. They dug below the water line along the bank and built wide hollow brick-lined columns that looked like wells. The sand was emptied from inside these wells till they hit solid earth and the wells were then filled with broken bricks, limestone and other rubble. Piers were erected on these wells at close intervals and joined with vaults above. A series of arches, rising above the piers supports the superstructure of the platform and holds up this platform to this day, 390 years after it was built,' explained Amma.

'How clever!' said Shiv.

'Excavation undertaken in the 1950s revealed wells filled with debris. The foundation of the Taj proved to be so stable that they did not give way, even during massive floods that occurred in 1978, when the river swelled, and the water level almost reached the top of the platform.'

Shiv and Veer were listening intently.

'Let me ask you a question,' said Amma. 'What do you think the Taj Mahal is made of?'

'Marble, duh!' quipped Veer.

'Not really,' said Amma and smiled. 'Contrary to popular belief, all buildings of the Taj complex are built of brick and then encrusted with white marble or sandstone slabs. These were locked together using iron clamps.'

Shiv and Veer looked surprised.

'The bricks were fired in kilns near Agra so transporting them to the construction site would be easy. The bricks used in Mughal buildings were all of a standard size, about seven inches long, four and a half inches wide and one and a half inches thick.

The red sandstone, called *sang-i-surkh* came mostly from quarries in Fatehpur Sikri, some 40 km to the west of Agra, while the white marble, called *sang-i-marmar* came from much further away from quarries near Jaipur in Rajasthan, more than 400 kilometres by road. Shah Jahan acquired the marble from Jai Singh, the Raja of Jaipur. An imperial instruction dated 20 September 1632 from Shah Jahan to Raja Jai Singh commands the Raja to deliver the marble to Agra.'

'Is he the same Raja Jai Singh from whom Shah Jahan got the land to build the Taj Mahal?' asked Veer.

'I'm glad you've been listening,' beamed Amma.

'Hundreds of carts pulled by water buffalos and bullocks laden with slabs of sandstone and white marble must have rumbled along the dusty roads to Agra, where thousands of builders and masons turned the bricks, mortar, rubble and stone into building walls, domes and pavement. The Yamuna river, too, was used to ferry wood, lime and other construction material in barges.

The marble slabs were heavy, and some of them were of such unusual size and length that they drew the sweat of many powerful teams of oxen, fierce looking, big-horned buffaloes, in teams of twenty or thirty animals, pulling specially constructed wagons.

As the building of the mausoleum progressed, the marble and other materials had to be lifted high up on to the scaffoldings. Usually, these scaffoldings were made of wood, but at the time, wood was in scarce supply and so the scaffolding was constructed using bricks instead. A system of beams, ropes and pulleys powered by men, oxen and even elephants were used to hoist the stones up to where they were to be fitted. Heavy ropes were used to secure the stones while they were being lifted, and for the heaviest blocks, metal lifting claws were inserted into pre-cut holes in the marble. Once the blocks reached the required height, the masons employed metal crowbars to fit them into place.

There is an interesting story about the scaffolding of bricks. When the construction was finished, Shah Jahan was told that it would take five years to remove the scaffolding. The clever emperor announced that those who dismantled the scaffolding could keep the bricks and apparently the scaffolding miraculously came down in a matter of days.'

'Very clever!' said Shiv.

'Yes indeed! Just like you get time to play on the PS4 if you finish your homework!' said Amma with a smile.

'We don't know the names of the stonemasons who worked on the construction of the Taj Mahal, but they made their contribution known through marks they scratched into the paving of the garden walkways and the slabs facing the walls of the buildings.'

'What do you mean Amma?' asked Veer looking confused.

'The stonemasons worked in groups called guilds. Each guild had its own history, skills and techniques that had been passed through generations. Guild members took pride in their work which they marked with unique signatures—geometric shapes such as triangles and squares, arrows, flowers and other symbols. Another reason was that the masons were paid for the amount of stone they cut and installed, and so marking their work was the best way to establish the amount they were owed.'

'How original!' said Veer.

'We'll walk along the garden walls later and you can spot the symbols,' said Amma.

Shiv and Veer nodded eagerly.

'With the foundation in place, work began on the platform and the main mausoleum, the Rauza. In Persia and Central Asia octagonal ground plans were commonly used in buildings. For the Taj Mahal, the architects chose the shape of a cube for the mausoleum building, measuring 180 square feet, with its vertical corners chamfered , or cut in a specific way, to produce an octagon. The cenotaph to mark the empress's grave was placed in a central octagonal shaped hall, surrounded by eight inter-connecting rooms on each of the two levels. This design embodies the sacred metaphor of *hasht-bihisht*, the eight principal gates and spaces of paradise, as believed in Islam.

Come, let's enter the mausoleum,' said Amma and the three walked ahead till they stood under the monumental arched doorway, the entrance to the tomb chamber.

The porch was accentuated by large inscriptions on its rectangular frame, written in a flowing script. The letters in black marble inscribed on the white marble walls of the mausoleum, looked spectacular. The high arch within the frame was topped by an inlaid flower. The spandrels—the triangular spaces between the tops of two adjacent arches—were filled with ornamental designs of flowers, called arabesques, in red, green and dark yellow.

'Do you see the inscriptions above?' asked Amma.

Shiv and Veer nodded.

'These are passages selected from the Quran, and were inscribed by one of the most accomplished calligraphers of the time, Abd ul-Haq who came to be known as Amanat Khan. Amanat Khan came to India in 1608, from Shiraz, Persia, and was appointed by Jahangir to work on the calligraphy that decorates Akbar's tomb. He was responsible for the calligraphy at the Taj Mahal and the selection of the verses from the Quran that adorn the monument.

He is the only artist whose name appears in the monument, although many talented craftsmen worked on the mausoleum. He signed the gateway that we entered from, in 1648, indicating its completion in that year.'

'Why is that Amma?'asked Veer.

'Calligraphy was the most respected skill in the Islamic world. After the death of Prophet Mohammad, his words were consolidated into probably the first and the finest book ever written in the Arabic language, the Quran. Quotations from the Quran became the chief decoration for mosques, and the perfection of the script became a high art. The calligrapher when transcribing the Quran, was repeating the word of God,' explained Amma.

'Can you look at the size of the letters carefully?' asked Amma looking at the calligraphy inscribed on the frame of the porch. 'This is another optical illusion. The size of the letters looks the same to you from here, does it not?'

Shiv and Veer nodded.

'If you look carefully, the size of the letters actually increases from the bottom to the top in a pre-calculated manner so that, to the eye of the beholder standing below, the size of the letters seems consistent over the whole arch.'

'That's right!' said Shiv, in wonder.

'The verses are written in the *thuluth* script, which Amanat Khan had a penchant for. This script was developed in Persia in the late ninth century. *Thuluth* means one third and it is so called because the proportion of the curved lines to the straight ones is precisely one third.

The funny thing is that while we know who the calligrapher was, we don't really know for sure who the architect of this grand structure was.'

'Why is that?' asked Veer.

'Well, I think maybe because this was Shah Jahan's biggest project and he wanted to be remembered as its creator. It is believed that he personally supervised the building of the Taj Mahal, and worked closely with a team of talented architects who were experts in their profession. Shah Jahan held daily meetings with them, and went over every detail of the work, giving structure to his vision of his queen's final resting place.

Most historians seem to agree that Ustad Ahmad Lahauri, was one of the creators of the Taj Mahal. Born in Lahore, Ustad Ahmad was not only a renowned architect but also a mathematician and astronomer of repute at the time. Lahauri's assistant was Ismail Effendi, who was from Turkey. He specialized in domes, like the one you see here. Chiranji Lal, a famous designer of mosaic patterns, hailed from Delhi, while Amir Ali, a master stone cutter and Mohammed Hanif, an expert in working with marble tiles arrived from Multan.

The entirety of the Taj Mahal is designed to evoke the vision of heaven or paradise as it was believed to exist in Islam and you can see that in many details here. The verses inscribed on the white marble panels of the gate and the monument are among the most profound passages in the Quran that speak of paradise. The symbolism of the gardens represent paradise, and the creation of flowers using precious stones, in accordance with Islamic tradition, symbolize the kingdom of God.'

The three stepped into the mausoleum and entered the tomb chamber. A hush fell among them. Even the smallest of sounds hung in the air, amplified and echoed across the vast hall and the high domed ceiling. Hundreds of decorative stone flowers and vines appeared to be woven across every surface. Motifs of flowers in vases, delicate lilies, irises and tulips, their leaves and petals delicately outlined, were engraved on the walls of the chamber. The floor, too, was paved with geometrical patterns of black marble, inlaid in white. Dim light filtered through the carved marble window screens.

The cenotaph of Mumtaz Mahal lay in the centre of the burial chamber, directly beneath the dome, with the larger cenotaph of Shah Jahan to the right. A white enclosure made of delicately perforated marble surrounded the tombs. The cenotaph was inlaid with bright, bejewelled flowers and flowery arabesques. The shimmering reflections of the gems set in pale marble created an unmatched splendour.

Amma spoke in a soft voice, 'The actual tombs of Mumtaz Mahal and Shah Jahan lie below, where they are buried in simple coffins.'

'Why is that Amma?' asked Veer.

'False tombs prevented people from defiling the actual graves. Also, cenotaphs enabled artistic expression as Muslim tradition forbids decoration of the graves. Underground burials are in keeping with the directive that the body must rest directly in the earth, which is equivalent to a sacrament in Islam.

Let me tell you something interesting about the baluster, that tall vase-like post that you see,' pointed out Amma. 'When the mausoleum was being built, a balustrade–a decorative railing of balusters– made of gold enclosed the cenotaph of Mumtaz Mahal. It is believed that the emperor, fearing that it may get stolen, had it replaced with a baluster of marble, an imitation of the original one. The baluster took ten years to make and was completed in 1643 at a cost of fifty thousand rupees. A few years later, Aurangzeb sold the precious enclosure to raise money for the costly military campaigns he wanted to undertake. It was replaced by a replica in marble filigree design studded with semi-precious stones. This is what you see today.

The walls were decorated
with stunning carvings. Branches of
white jasmine, made of mother of pearl wound
around a red pomegranate flower of carnelian gemstone,
while delicate oleanders peeped out from under a rich green
foliage, every leaf, every petal was a separate emerald, pearl or topaz.

These flowers are beautiful. Don't they look real, as if we could reach out and touch them?' said Amma.

Veer reached out his hands to touch the carvings. Amma stopped him in time.

'You said we could touch the flowers,' said Veer with a naughty gleam in his eyes.

'I told you that visitors are not allowed to touch the walls,' scolded Amma 'Heritage monuments need special care.'

Amma, Shiv and Veer slowly walked around the marble screen, observing all the details.

'In the whole Mughal empire, there was no one more proficient in the knowledge of stones than Shah Jahan. You can see his passion for jewels in the variety of gems inlaid here as well as the attention to detail and fine finish. Over forty types of different gems were used. Shah Jahan had them transported from all over Asia—jade from China, deep blue, gold-flecked lapis lazuli from Afghanistan, turquoise from Tibet, coral from Arabia, yellow amber from Burma (modern-day Myanmar), deep green malachite from Russia and rubies from Sri Lanka.

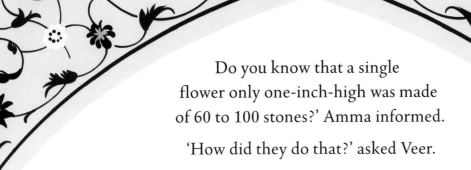

Do you know that a single flower only one-inch-high was made of 60 to 100 stones?' Amma informed.

'How did they do that?' asked Veer.

'Artists used a special technique called *parchin kari*, which means "inlay" to make these flowers. First, the craftsmen would use a grinding wheel to carve the shape of the flower on the marble wall. Next, they polished the stones and cut them to size with a small bow saw, to fit into the hollow spaces. A special kind of glue was used to hold the pieces in place. The surface of the flower was polished so that the lines between the stones became invisible.

Some claim that *parchin kari* comes from the Italian hard stone inlay work called pietra dura, which was practised in Florence. Historians say that travellers from Europe brought this art to India. Others say that long before the Europeans arrived, Indians had developed the technique of *parchin kari*, which was used for calligraphy and decoration. It is quite likely that the Europeans or the objects they brought with them to the imperial court as gifts influenced

Shah Jahan and his craftsmen to extend *parchin kari* to incorporate the jewels so beloved to the emperor.'

A huge, beautiful bronze lamp inlaid with gold and silver hung above the cenotaphs.

Amma looked up and spoke softly, 'This lamp was a gift from Lord Curzon, the Viceroy and Governor General of India, appointed by the British in 1899.

Shah Jahan had organised funding for the upkeep of the Taj Mahal even after his death, but by the late 1700s, it fell into neglect and parts of the mausoleum were damaged. In the next two hundred years, the Taj Mahal was further damaged and was also looted by marauding groups as the Mughal empire and its influence started to decline.

Lord Curzon was horrified to see the degree of neglect at the Taj Mahal and ordered a complete restoration of the complex. Precious stones that had been stolen from the inlays were replaced, cracks in the minarets were repaired and the marble facade was cleaned. The trees in the gardens had overgrown such that one could barely see the monument as one entered from the Great Gate. The gardens were restored and younger trees were planted and regularly trimmed. The water channels were revived and flowerbeds planted. For years, Curzon visited the Taj Mahal regularly, constantly checking that his orders were being carried out. While he was viceroy (1899-1905), an amount of 50,000 pounds was spent on restoring the Taj Mahal.

The original chandelier was damaged, so Lord Curzon commissioned a renowned Egyptian artist, Todros Badir, to make another one, a copy of the lamp that had hung in the mosque of Sultan Beybars II in Cairo. This was undertaken at Curzon's own expense and was made of copper, inlaid with gold and silver work and took two years to complete. Curzon had a dedication inscribed on the lamp, "Presented to the tomb of Mumtaz Mahal by Lord Curzon, Viceroy 1906", in Persian, so that it would be in harmony with the great tomb it intended to illuminate.

The lamp was installed on February 16, 1908, at an event attended by a vast congregation, where a message from Lord Curzon, who was no longer in India, was read out. "In asking you to see to its final installation, I would beg that it be carefully guarded by the custodians of the shrine and may hang there as my last tribute to the glories of Agra which float like a vision of eternal beauty in my memory." Lord Curzon said that saving the Taj Mahal was his greatest achievement.

The bench that we sat on in the gardens and the other benches that you saw, were instated on the orders of Lord Curzon in 1907,' said Amma.

'As part of an effort to preserve India's heritage, the British government founded the Archaeological Survey of India in 1860. This organisation continues even today and is tasked with the conservation and preservation of all historical and cultural monuments in India, including the Taj Mahal.'

After completing the walk around the mausoleum hall, Amma and the boys came out to the massive terrace, and made their way to the back of the mausoleum that overlooked the River Yamuna. The floor of the terrace was paved with geometrical patterns of lighter and darker sandstone slabs and marble. A gentle cool breeze blew across the river on to the terrace.

'Let's stand there for a while,' said Amma walking towards the edge of the terrace. Shiv and Veer followed as Amma leaned over the brink of the terrace wall and pointed to stone steps leading up from the riverbank.

Though Shah Jahan had carefully planned every step of the visitors' walk from the Great Gate, the garden complex, up to this terrace and into the mausoleum, it was not a walk he usually took himself. Instead, he travelled across the river by boat and climbed these steps from the river's edge to get here.'

The three were quiet for a while, gazing at the tranquil waters of the Yamuna.

'You both wanted to know how much money it took to build the Taj Mahal. Can you take a guess?' asked Amma.

Shiv and Veer shrugged their shoulders.

'It cost 32 million rupees by the time work was finished in its entirety,' said Amma. 'If the Taj Mahal were to be built today it would cost 70,000 crores in rupees or 1 billion US dollars.'

'Wow!' exclaimed Shiv and gasped.

'Where did the money to build the Taj Mahal come from?' asked Veer.

'From the treasury of the emperor,' said Amma. 'He was the richest man in the world, after all! He also arranged for ongoing funding for the upkeep of the Taj such that one third of the amount came from tax revenues collected from the 30 villages surrounding Agra. Two-thirds came from the tax paid on the income of the bazaars and inns outside the Taj Mahal complex.'

Amma pointed across the Yamuna river, that shone like a sheet of silver below them. 'Can you see that large patch of green on the bank across the river?' she asked.

Shiv and Veer nodded.

'Till a few years ago, a huge mound of sand stood in its place. The winds would blow the sand across the river and the sand particles would rub against and damage the white marble walls of the mausoleum. To protect the Taj from this, the Archaeological Survey of India decided to excavate the mound and level out the land in the 1990s. As they started the excavation, they made a startling discovery. Buried under the mounds of sand they found traces of a large garden, the remains of a water system along with remnants of pavilions. The most interesting discovery was a huge octagonal pool with twenty-four fountains exactly like the one we saw in the gardens of the Taj.'

'Wow. Whose garden was this?' asked Shiv.

'Historians say that the garden was originally built by Babur. Over the years the garden came into the possession of Raja Man Singh and when Shah Jahan acquired this land from him; the gardens across the bank of the Yamuna came along with it. The garden was known as 'Mahtab Bagh' which means 'moonlit garden'. They were at a lower level than the Taj and therefore may have been flooded by the river, which is what probably led to them being abandoned, as early as the seventeenth century,' explained Amma.

'Historians say that Mahtab Bagh was integral to the design of the Taj Mahal,' said Amma.

'How so, Amma?' asked Shiv.

'The garden is perfectly aligned with the gardens of the Taj Mahal. Shah Jahan had lined up the Taj Mahal complex and Mahtab Bagh in such a way that Mumtaz Mahal's great tomb would have sat perfectly in the middle of the two gardens if there had been no river in between. That makes sense as the common design for Mughal mausoleums is at the centre of surrounding symmetrical gardens instead of standing at one end of a garden as the Taj appears to be. Isn't that fascinating?

Mahtab Bagh was designed to be enjoyed at night; a garden full of white flowers that released their fragrance in the cool evening air. The most prominent feature of the garden was the octagonal pool, which was positioned to reflect the Taj in its waters. You can imagine Shah Jahan standing there on a moonlit night, enjoying the scent of the gardens and the cooling mist from the fountains as he gazed upon his perfect creation and its shimmering reflection in the waters of the pool,' said Amma wistfully.

'I want to go to Mahtab Bagh and see the Taj Mahal from there!' said Shiv eagerly.

'The garden has been restored recently and we can indeed go there later. But let me tell you the rest of the story about Shah Jahan,' said Amma and carried on.

'In 1638, before the construction of the Taj Mahal was completed, Shah Jahan decided to move the empire's capital to Delhi, as Agra had become overcrowded. He instructed his engineers and architects to build an enormous brand new city that he called Shahjahanabad, or the City of Shah Jahan. He moved the entire imperial court to his new city in 1648 leaving his beloved Taj Mahal behind. But he did return to Agra every year for Mumtaz Mahal's *Urs* ceremony.

In 1657, an ageing Shah Jahan fell seriously ill, and it was feared that he would not live for very long. On hearing the news of their father's illness, Shah Jahan's four sons, in true Mughal fashion, started planning and plotting their way to ascend the Mughal throne. Shah Jahan, himself favoured his eldest son, Dara Shikoh, whom he had declared as his heir apparent. But even as Shah Jahan started to recover from his illness, a war of succession broke out between his sons. The bloody conflict would last for a year and would end with Aurengzeb, Shah Jahan's third son, defeating the armies of his brothers and crowning himself as the new Mughal emperor in 1658 even though his father was still alive to rule. He had the frail Shah Jahan confined to quarters at the Agra Fort and cruelly sent him the severed head of Dara Shikoh who had been executed a few months back on his brother's orders.'

Shiv and Veer gasped.

'Remember when I said that Shah Jahan's actions when he succeeded his own father would come back to haunt him? They surely did. Shah Jahan would live the last seven years of his life as a prisoner in a marble-walled jail, friendless and in failing health.

He spent his days reading the Quran and gazing out of a window across the Yamuna river at the Taj Mahal. Jahanara, his daughter, who after Mumtaz Mahal's death had been his constant companion, shared her father's imprisonment and cared for him during this time.'

'That's so sad, Amma,' said Veer.

'Yes, Veer, it is,' said Amma. 'Shah Jahan had to pay the price for what he had done to his own brothers many decades earlier. Our actions have consequences, which we cannot escape from and there is a lesson for all of us in this sad story,' said Amma.

'The imprisoned Shah Jahan was not even allowed to visit the tomb of his wife, the paradise for Mumtaz Mahal that he had so lovingly conceived and created. In January 1666, shortly after his 74th birthday, Shah Jahan breathed his last. It is believed that he died in his bed, looking at a mirror so placed that it reflected the Taj Mahal. His body was moved to the burial chamber beneath the mausoleum and was placed next to the grave of Mumtaz Mahal, uniting the lovers after 30 years. Above, in the main chamber, a second white marble cenotaph was added to mark the new grave below, the only discordant note in an otherwise perfectly symmetrical layout.

Shah Jahan's growing court, his vast building projects, his costly jewels drained the Mughal treasury faster than his tax collectors could replenish it. The empire that Aurangzeb seized from his father in 1658 had started a decline that would never be reversed. Even though Aurangzeb succeeded in further expanding the empire's borders, after his death, Mughal rule grew weaker and weaker. Mughal emperors ruled for another 82 years, but the time of their greatness was over.'

Amma and the boys had spent a long time on the terrace of the Taj Mahal. They walked around the mausoleum and retraced their steps, walking through the lush gardens till they stood at the same place where they had first set sights on the gleaming mausoleum.

The Taj Mahal shone bright under the hot afternoon sun, the mausoleum dominating the skyline, its reflection rippling in the waters, riveting the eye and the mind.

Shiv and Veer were silent, gazing at the beauty of the monument for one last time.

'There are many things that are special about the Taj Mahal—its grandeur, its imposing gate, the long approach to the monument, the wide paths, the size of the tomb and its unearthly appearance above the high platform, the lustrous marble and the jewelled decorations. The mausoleum is a product of the labour of thousands of people who conceived, designed and worked hard to create one of the world's best-known monuments.

But, do you know what is most special about the Taj Mahal, for me?' asked Amma. 'That it is a memorial of love of a king for his queen. It is above all, born out of deep emotion. At the heart of all the grandeur and magnificence, lie two people who loved each other deeply.

I am reminded of a poem that the great poet and philosopher Rabindranath Tagore wrote on the Taj Mahal,' said Amma.

'You knew, Emperor of India, Shah Jahan,

That life, youth, wealth, renown

All float away down the stream of time…

Yet still one solitary tear

Would hang on the cheek of time

In the form

Of this white and gleaming Taj Mahal.'

The three took once last glance at the Taj Mahal and made their way out.

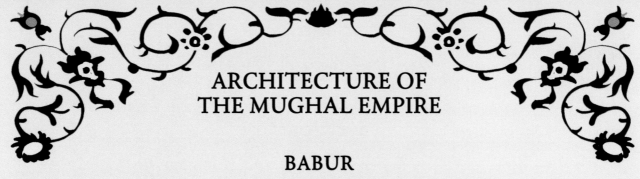

ARCHITECTURE OF
THE MUGHAL EMPIRE

BABUR
(1483–1530) reigned 1526–1530

Gardens at Agra

HUMAYUN
(1530–1556) reigned 1530–1540; 1555–1556

Sabz Burj in Delhi
Mausoleum of Sher Shah
Library in Purana Qila in Delhi
Qila-i-Kuhna Masjid in Delhi

AKBAR
(1542–1605) reigned 1556–1605

Mausoleum of Humayun
Red Fort at Agra
Fatehpur Sikri

JAHANGIR
(1605–1627) reigned 1605–1627

Mausoleum of Akbar at Sikandra
Mausoleum of Itimad-ud-Daulah in Agra
Mausoleum of Abdur Rahim Khan i-Khanan in Delhi

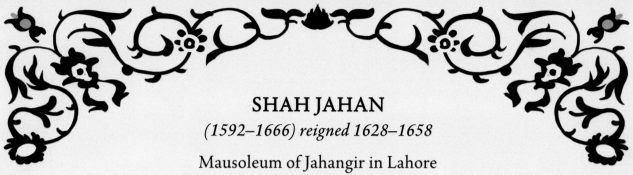

SHAH JAHAN
(1592–1666) reigned 1628–1658

Mausoleum of Jahangir in Lahore
Palace in the fort at Agra
Jama Masjid in Agra
Sheesh Mahal
Taj Mahal
Sahali Burj (mausoleum near the Taj)

AURANGZEB
(1618–1707) reigned 1658–1707

BAHADUR SHAH
(1643–1712) reigned 1707–1712

FARRUKHSIYAR
(1683–1719) reigned 1713–1719

MUHAMMAD SHAH
(1702–1748) reigned 1719–1748

BAHADUR SHAH II
(1775–1862) reigned 1837–1857

END OF THE MUGHAL EMPIRE
1857

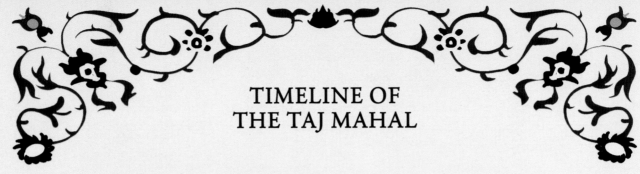

TIMELINE OF
THE TAJ MAHAL

1526   The Mughal empire is established. Babur wins the Battle of Panipat, defeats Ibrahim Lodi and becomes the emperor of India

1556   Akbar the Great becomes emperor

1592   Birth of Khurram, Shah Jahan

1607   Khurram meets Mumtaz Mahal

1612   Khurram and Mumtaz Mahal are wed

1631   Mumtaz Mahal dies

1632   Construction of the Taj Mahal begins

1648   The Taj Mahal is completed

1658   Aurangzeb displaces his father, becomes emperor

1666   Shah Jahan dies

1707 Aurangzeb dies

1877 Queen Victoria becomes Empress of India

1899 Lord Curzon begins reviving the Taj complex

1947 India gains independence

1983 The Taj Mahal is declared a
      UNESCO World Heritage Site

1990 Remnants of Mehtab Bagh (Moonlight
      Garden) discovered on the other side of the river

1996 India's Supreme Court orders anti-pollution
      measures to protect the building from deterioration

1999 Indo-Pakistan war, Taj is camouflaged

2007 Chosen as one of the New Seven Wonders of the
      World by millions of voters from around the world

INTERESTING FACTS

- The Taj Mahal attracts seven to eight million visitors every year, with over 40,000 to 50,000 visitors on a single day, at times.

- UNESCO World Heritage classifies the Taj Mahal as one of the 'Seven Wonders of the World'.

- The Taj Mahal is closed to the public on Fridays.

- To protect the Taj Mahal from potential bombing during World War II and later wars, the monument was concealed by extensive scaffolding so that it is not recognisable from the air.

- An environmentally clean area of 4,000-square-miles has been established around the Taj Mahal. There is a ban on petrol and diesel vehicles driving within 500 metres of the monument. Visitors must walk or take electric buses to access the mausoleum. These measures are to protect the Taj Mahal from the harmful effects of air pollution.

SELECTED BIBLIOGRAPHY

Beveridge, Annette Susannah, trans. *Baburnama*. New Delhi: Rupa Publications, 2017.

Dalrymple, William, and Anita Anand. Kohinoor: *The Story of the World's Most Infamous Diamond*. New Delhi: Juggernaut Books, 2016.

Eraly, Abraham. Emperors of the Peacock Throne: *The Saga of the Great Mughals*. New Delhi: Penguin Books, 2000.

————. The Mughal World: *India's Tainted Paradise*. London: Orion Books, 2008.

Gascoigne, Bamber. *The Great Moghuls: India's Most Flamboyant Rulers*. London: Robinson, 2002.

Grewal, Royina. *In the Shadow of The Taj: A Portrait of Agra*. New Delhi: Rupa Publications, 2014.

Hoobler, Dorothy, Thomas Hoobler, and John Hinderliter. *Where is the Taj Mahal?* New York: Penguin Random House, 2017.

Hourly History. *Taj Mahal: A History from Beginning to Present*. California: Createspace Independent Publishing Platform, 2018.

Koch, Ebba. *Mughal Architecture: An Outline of its History and Development*. Delhi: Primus Books, 2002.

Koch, Ebba, and Richard André Barraud. *The Complete Taj Mahal and the Riverfront Gardens of Agra*. London: Thames and Hudson, 2006.

Mann, Elizabeth. *Taj Mahal: A Story of Love and Empire*. New York: Miyaka Press, 2008.

Moynihan, Elizabeth B. *Paradise as a Garden: In Persia and Mughal India*. New York: George Braziller, 1979.

————. *The Moonlight Gardens: New Discoveries at the Taj Mahal*. Washington D.C.: Smithsonian Institution, 2000.

Murari, Timeri N. *Taj: A Story of Mughal India*. New Delhi: Penguin Books, 1985.

Preston, Diana, and Michael Preston. *A Teardrop on the Cheek of Time: The Story of the Taj Mahal*. London: Doubleday, 2007.

Richards, John F. *The Mughal Empire*. Cambridge: Cambridge University Press, 1993.

Sharma, Parvati. *Jahangir: An Intimate Portrait of a Great Mughal*. New Delhi: Juggernaut Books, 2018.

Sharma, Parvati, and Urmimala Nag. *The Story of Babur*, New Delhi: Goodearth Pvt. Ltd; Puffin Books, 2015.

Sundaresan, Indu. *The Mountain of Light*. New Delhi: HarperCollins Publishers India, 2013.

READ MORE IN THE SERIES

AMMA TAKE ME TO THE GOLDEN TEMPLE

Join Amma and her children as they travel to the Golden Temple in Amritsar, the holiest seat of Sikhism. Take a tour through Harmandir Sahib. Hear inspiring stories about the Sikh gurus. Enjoy the langar offered by the world's biggest kitchen. Learn Guru Nanak's eternal message of equality, love and sacrifice.

AMMA TAKE ME TO TIRUPATI

Follow Amma and the boys to the world-famous temple of Tirupati Balaji. Listen to the captivating lore about a snake that became a hill range and how Vishnu came to reside on the very same hillock. Wake up to the hymns of Suprabhatam. Savour the delicious Tirupati ladoo and witness the adoration of Venkateshwara's devotees.

AMMA TAKE ME TO THE DARGAH OF SALIM CHISHTI

Travel with Amma and her boys to the fortress city of Fatehpur Sikri. Hear the story of why the great Mughal emperor Akbar visited the Sufi saint Salim Chishti and had a mausoleum built in his honour. Behold the dargah, shining like a white pearl in an oasis of red sandstone.

AMMA TAKE ME TO SHIRDI

Join Amma and her boys as they travel to Shirdi, home to one of India's most celebrated, loved and revered saints – Sai Baba. Walk around the neem tree that gave him shelter. Relish a few moments in Dwarka Mai, the dilapidated mosque that became his home. Visit Dhuni Mai, the ever-burning fire that Sai Baba had lit, and receive his blessings.